DIGGING DEEPER

Excavating medieval houses, the Close, Newcastle.

DIGGING DEEPER

The origins of Newcastle and Gateshead

David Heslop and Zoë McAuley

Tyne Bridge Publishing

Acknowledgements

The authors and Tyne Bridge Publishing would like to thank the following for their invaluable assistance in the production of Digging Deeper:

Lindsay Allason-Jones, Richard Annis, Ian Ayris, Richard Bailey, Tony Ball, Paul Bidwell, Suzanne Caldicott, Emma Carter, Judith Dobie, Anthony Flowers, Pam Graves, John Grundy, Barbara Harbottle, Vanessa Histon, Jaqui Huntley, Anthea Lang, Geoff Laws, Tony Liddell, John Mabbitt, Clare McCrae, Paul McDonald, Jonathan McKelvey, Jenny Morrison, John Nolan, Andrew Parkin, Jamie Quartermain, Jenny Vaughan; Archaeological Services Durham University, North Pennines Archaeology, Northern Counties Archaeological Service, Oxford Archaeology North, Ryders Architecture, Society of Antiquaries of Newcastle upon Tyne, Tyne & Wear Archives and Museums.

Photographs are © of Newcastle City Council unless otherwise indicated.

Many of the objects illustrated in Digging Deeper are on display at the Great North Museum/Hancock, and at the Castle Keep, Newcastle upon Tyne.

Cover design: Anthony Flowers

Cover image: The Castle Keep during restoration, c.1812

Back cover photograph: Clavering Place, 2009

© David Heslop and Zoë McAuley, 2011

ISBN: 978 185795 134 9

Published by
City of Newcastle upon Tyne
Newcastle Libraries & Information Service
Tyne Bridge Publishing, 2011

www.tynebridgepublishing.co.uk
www.newcastle.gov.uk/libraries

ISBN: 978-1-85795-205-6

Printed by Elanders UK Ltd, North Tyneside

TWAM

Bronze Age collared urn found with a burial at Rye Hill, Newcastle. On display at the Great North Museum.

A FOREWORD BY JOHN GRUNDY

On the wall of the Neville Hall at the bottom of Westgate Road, is a plaque marking the route of Hadrian's Wall. I love that plaque. I love to be reminded that as the modern city roars on past, the Roman Wall still lurks beneath our feet. And not just the Roman Wall; just off Pilgrim Street the remains of a Bronze Age house were recently discovered; there's a Roman town buried behind the station and a Saxon cemetery underneath the Castle – indeed the Norman builders desecrated the cemetery, arrogantly laying the foundation of their walls among the scattered bones of their defeated enemy. And beneath all the later layers, there are tantalising glimpses of the earliest human history of all – the stone age people who probably lived here five or six thousand years ago. As the Sage Gateshead was being built, two vast ditches emerged which may be the remains of a ceremonial henge monument overlooking the great River Tyne.

As David Heslop says, it was the river that started it all. The earliest inhabitants used it and worshipped it. Bronze Age Geordies hurled beautifully

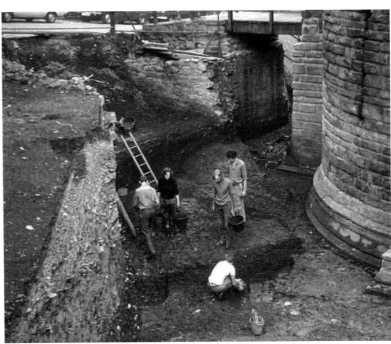

Excavations in the defensive moat of the Black Gate, in the 1970s. The finds among rubbish thrown into the moat provide some of our best information about life in the Middle Ages.

5

worked swords into it as part of some act of religious veneration and the Romans came here because it was the first place they could easily and safely build a bridge. Their bridge was named Pons Aelius, one of only two bridges in the Roman Empire named after Emperors, the other led across the Tiber in Rome to the vast Mausoleum which Hadrian built for himself. I love that story too because it suggests that even in Roman times Tyneside was important in the way that Geordies know it is today.

This is not yet a complete story. The complete story is buried beneath the walls and roads of a vibrant modern city and the distant past emerges gradually and almost by accident. Recently a 1960s concrete garage was demolished on Melbourne Street and lo ... the Roman Wall emerged from beneath the floor – another piece of the ancient jigsaw fell into place. It really is so exciting that so many of the discoveries in this book have only come to light in the last decade. It makes you wonder what might be revealed tomorrow ...

John Grundy, September 2011

Courtesy Archaeological Services Durham University

Hadrian's Wall was unexpectedly discovered in 2003 beneath the foundations of a garage on Melbourne Street, Newcastle. This part of the wall, between Newcastle and Wallsend, was added at a slightly later date than the original phase from Newcastle to Carlisle.

OLD FATHER TYNE

The River God Tyne (David Wynne, 1968) looks down from a wall of the Civic Centre, Newcastle.

Before everything was the river. Not the deep and fast-flowing river restrained by quay walls of steel and concrete we see today, but the ancient river, which was shallow and broad and which could be forded at low tide. The whole story of the origins of human settlement at Newcastle and Gateshead can be brought back to the importance of the river. It was a source of food, water and raw materials and a boundary for the tribal clans living on either side. It was also a route-way through the landscape, from the coastline deep inland into the fells of the Pennines. At a deeper level, the river was seen both as a living force in the form of a river god and as a gateway to the spirit world. Passing through the water led to a realm every bit as real in the imagination of our ancestors as the landscape of woods, fields and villages that they could see and touch all around them.

The full story of the earliest settlements on the banks of the river Tyne is being slowly uncovered through excavation and by researching the objects stored in museums. It is a history that changes with every new find. As advances in archaeological sciences and genetics challenge our long-held beliefs about who we are, and where we came from, so our understanding of the origins of Newcastle and Gateshead is growing and the past is being brought back to life.

This 1860s engraving of the Tyne at Elswick shows the wide and meandering river of long ago.

THE EARLIEST TIMES

Who were the first people to settle on the banks of the river Tyne? To answer that question we must look beyond present day Newcastle and Gateshead to discoveries across Tyneside and the wider region. No excavations in Tyne and Wear have so far revealed direct evidence of the settlers of the Neolithic period, the first people in the region to build permanent homes in a farming landscape. At Yeavering and Thirlings in Northumberland, traces of the rectangular timber houses of these simple farming communities have been found. Almost as soon as they were growing crops, the people gathered to build banked and ditched enclosures to meet each other and worship the gods – one of the earliest monumental religious sites is at Milfield near Wooler. They date to between 4,000 and 2,000 BC.

Further south, great Neolithic monuments have been found at crossing points of the major rivers that flow from the Pennines into the North Sea. Some of these places, like the Devil's Arrows at Boroughbridge, Catterick Henge on the river Swale and the Thornborough Henges, are so large that many people would have been needed to drag the stones or build the banks. Large numbers of people would also have been able to fit inside the monuments, which may have acted as open-air amphitheatres. People lived in small villages at this time, so the builders would have travelled great distances to gather and work together at these places.

Geoff Laws

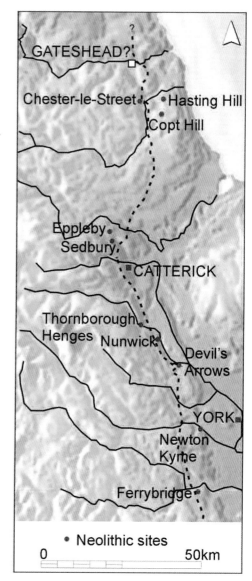

Neolithic ceremonial sites located on or near the Great North Road.

Left, neolithic perforated stone battle axe.

In 2001 two large ditches of a massive enclosure were found beneath St Mary's church, revealed during the building of the Sage Gateshead. Further work would be needed to confirm the date of the site. The scattered communities may have gathered at such places to celebrate annual festivals and perform important rituals to appease the gods and make the crops grow. These festivals provided opportunities for farmers and their families to meet and do the trading necessary for the isolated farmsteads to survive.

It is a mistake to think of these early farmers as self sufficient – most farms would need to acquire a wide range of essential goods, like cutting implements, salt and grinding stones. Just as vital were husbands and wives from outside the family, and farm animals to replace those lost to predators and disease. By building up family connections with communities both near and far, a kinship network was created and social events, linked to the religious calendar, maintained the family bonds through the generations. Each group now had a safety net if they needed help in times of hardship. The river provided a link to all of the groups along the fertile Tyne valley, and at Newcastle it was crossed by the ancient road to the north and south.

Excavations carried out at Robson's Yard during the building of the Sage Gateshead, revealed traces of what may be a Neolithic causewayed enclosure. The two-half-sectioned parallel ditches may date to the prehistoric period. The large semi-circular pit in the foreground is probably a medieval coal-working pit.

THE CUTTING EDGE

The earliest Neolithic artefacts have been found along the river banks – the stone and flint axes that were the tools that Neolithic farmers needed to cut back the wild woodland. The hard, fine-grained stone required to make such axes is found in only a few places, such as at the Great Langdale axe factory near Ambleside, Cumbria where they were made in large numbers. These axes would be carried along the ancient routes, like the Stainmore Pass over the Pennines, finding their way as far as East Yorkshire, Lincolnshire and the East Midlands. They were traded for other items at the great meeting places. The banks of the Tyne would have been a perfect location for such an assembly.

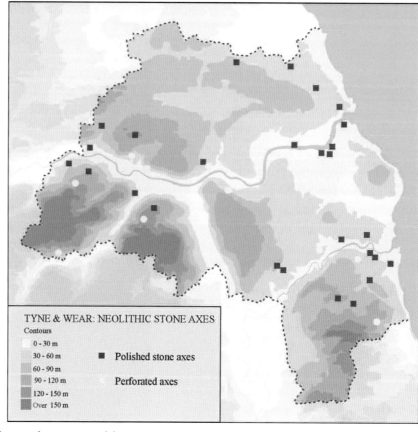

TYNE & WEAR: NEOLITHIC STONE AXES

Contours
0 - 30 m
30 - 60 m
60 - 90 m
90 - 120 m
120 - 150 m
Over 150 m

■ Polished stone axes

○ Perforated axes

The axes would continue to change hands for centuries to come, though their meaning would also change. They seem to have been collected as novelties in the Roman period, but by then they were believed to be the thunderbolts of Zeus. In the Middle Ages, some fossils were thought to be the tips of petrified thunderbolts and were kept for luck. The beautiful stone axe (right) was found in the Roman fort in Newcastle and may be an example of such a lucky object. If that is the case, it could have moved across the Empire, among the personal belongings of a Roman soldier or official.

Right, a polished stone axe head from the Roman fort.

CLUES IN THE EARTH

We have not yet located the settlements of the Neolithic period, but it is possible to assess the environmental impact of the first prehistoric farmers. We can study the ecology of the Neolithic landscape by examining pollen grains, which are preserved in peat bogs and other waterlogged sites.

Palynology is the study of pollen as a means of reconstructing past environments. Pollen is extremely hardy and so can be preserved indefinitely in waterlogged places with oxygen-free sediments. By examining the grains collected during excavations through a microscope, plant species can be identified. From the proportion of each species found from different habitats (woodland, grassland, ploughlands etc) we can work out the ecology and environment created by our ancestors.

The pollen profiles tell us that between 10,000 and 4,000 BC the population began to clear small areas of forest to create fields, but by the end of the Neolithic period more farmland was needed to support the growing population. For the first time, British forests began to be permanently reduced by large-scale clearances. The pollen dating from this time changes, with mature oak, elm, birch and alder being replaced by cereal crops and grassland for pasture.

TWAM

A rise in population led to more contact between people, and consequent competition for resources. The formidable piece of stonework, above left, was found in a drain near St Thomas' Church, Barras Bridge, in 1893. When in use, it would have been mounted at the top of a wooden shaft. It has been called a 'battleaxe' as it is possible that this heavy implement was a weapon, rather than a tool.

The larger battleaxe on the right was found at Whickham, near Newcastle.

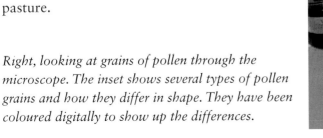

Courtesy English Heritage

Right, looking at grains of pollen through the microscope. The inset shows several types of pollen grains and how they differ in shape. They have been coloured digitally to show up the differences.

DEAD AND BURIED?

At a conservative estimate at least 30,000 people lived and died on Tyneside over the 2,000 years of the Neolithic period, but only a handful of burials dating to that period have been found. Some burial places may have been destroyed over the centuries and some have yet to be discovered, but we suspect most bodies must have been removed from the world of the living in a way that has left no trace today.

In the Neolithic period, communities buried their dead in 'barrows' made up of mounds of earth with chambers at their centre, where the bones were heaped. The fact that many burials consist of loose bones, with parts of the skeleton missing or mixed with those of other individuals, suggests that bodies were left for long periods before burial, allowing the flesh to decompose. Platforms for exposing bodies have been found on sites in Yorkshire and southern England. This process of 'excarnation', has been practised in India and by Native North Americans. It may have been regarded as freeing the spirit from the body through natural processes, giving the family time to grieve and to prepare the final ceremonies, which ended when the bones were sealed inside the barrow.

After about 2000 BC, at the beginning of the Bronze Age (around 2000-650 BC), a different

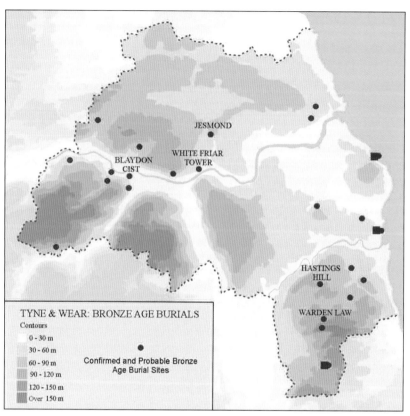

TYNE & WEAR: BRONZE AGE BURIALS

Contours

	0 - 30 m
	30 - 60 m
	60 - 90 m
	90 - 120 m
	120 - 150 m
	Over 150 m

● Confirmed and Probable Bronze Age Burial Sites

Warden Law, a Bronze Age burial site which uses a natural glacial mound which resembles a man-made barrow.

sort of burial becomes common. Smaller, circular barrows were constructed, and made more striking by being located on the crests of hills and other easily visible places. Individuals were buried in stone cists (a grave lined with stone slabs), along with objects such as bronze knives or jet buttons, which reflected social position and status.

A unique example of an Early Bronze Age burial in central Newcastle was recorded in 1841 when a grave lined with stone slabs was found during the demolition of the White Friar Tower (on the town walls, behind the Central Station), along with an urn. No bones were found, but the acidic soil conditions may have dissolved them. This was a high point above a river, a common place for Bronze Age burials. Better recorded examples are known from Jesmond and Blaydon.

During the Bronze Age the population probably increased so burial mounds or barrows became a more prominent feature in the landscape. Barrows have been found throughout Tyne and Wear but because of the lack of less visible features such as settlements we can still only account for a fraction of the population.

This is one of five burial cists found in Blaydon, all uncovered accidentally during the 1930s. Each of these stone-lined graves contained at least one skeleton and was sealed with a stone slab. Four contained a pottery beaker, while one had a flint knife.

In 1828, Mr Russell Blackbird unearthed a Bronze Age cist from his garden in Jesmond, Newcastle. It contained a well-preserved adult skeleton and this beautifully decorated bowl.

TRIBUTE TO THE RIVER GODS

In the middle of the 19th century Victorian engineers, in the process of improving the Tyne's navigability, dredged deeply into the river bed. They removed a staggering 90 million tons of sand and gravel from the river channel at Elswick, west of Newcastle, all the way to dumping grounds off the coast beyond Tynemouth. This great engineering feat accidentally stirred up finds from the town's distant past. Freed from the river bed, several bronze swords and spearheads were recovered by the dredging crews.

These works of ancient craftsmanship were made over 3,000 years ago when metal working was regarded as a magical act of creation, rather than an industrial process. The largest sword (far right) is a far-travelled and exotic piece, forged by a continental smith. The blades were passed on to local antiquarians, who imagined them to be the weapons and tools of Celtic warriors, cast aside in ancient battles along the riverside or lost from canoes and boats.

Now it seems probable such artefacts were deliberately placed in the river as offerings. Across much of north-western Europe major rivers have yielded similar finds, sometimes hundreds at a time. They were almost certainly part of a religious act, perhaps a tribute to the river spirits, in exchange for prosperity and protection. The practice of depositing high quality weaponry into rivers reappears in the Middle Ages and is preserved in the Arthurian legends, which conclude when the enchanted sword Excalibur is returned to the Lady of the Lake to complete the cycle of the story.

In the discovery of these blades we have the first certain evidence of the importance of the actual river crossing that would become the bridging point between Newcastle and Gateshead. What brought people here was a ford across the river, the best place that the Tyne could be crossed all year round. Such a spot is a classic example of the places that attracted Bronze Age and Iron Age offerings across Britain. Others include the shallow points along the Thames, the Witham and the Trent, where bronze weapons have been found. It is this ford that would draw the Romans, and after them the Normans, to settle here.

This might have been the scene on the riverbank moments before a Bronze Age sword was flung into the river. Without written accounts, it is impossible to know what rites were performed in prehistory, but giving up such a valuable item must have been a solemn and sacred event.

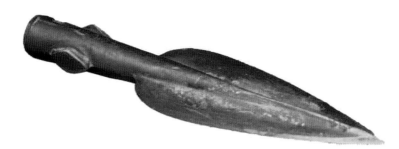

The bronze spear head above, and the sword, right, were found in the Tyne. It is likely that swords and other weapons (despite being rare and undoubtedly valuable possessions) were deposited in the river as offerings or a tribute to local gods.

SETTLEMENT IN THE DAYS BEFORE ROME

During a redevelopment on High Bridge in central Newcastle, archaeologists uncovered part of a curved trench. It was an exciting find and recognised as a type of trench used for the foundations of a Late Bronze Age hut, the earliest excavated evidence for a local population. Radio-carbon dating confirmed that it dated to 1500-800 BC. Wooden planks would have been placed upright in the trench to form the walls of a round hut supporting a cone-shaped thatched roof. It stood only 20m away from Pilgrim Street. This main thoroughfare, part of the Great North Road, may have been a roadway even then.

Just a few miles north of Newcastle City Centre, at Brunton, in a new housing development near Newcastle Airport, archaeologists have found the remains of Bronze Age and Iron Age villages, consisting of groups of round huts, surrounded by their fields and track-ways. They were in use from about 800 BC until shortly after the Roman Conquest. In these village sites, new houses were built on the sites of older houses repeatedly for centuries.

Courtesy Rising Sun Farm

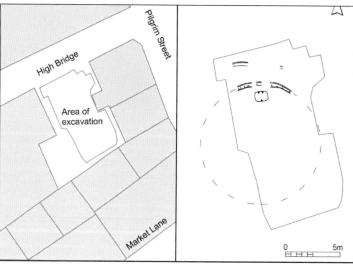

Tyne & Wear Historic Environment Record

Top, this replica round hut can be seen at Rising Sun Country Park. The Bronze Age hut at High Bridge (above) would have been very similar to this, the curving ditch (in red) showing the outline of the walls.

Left, the darker shapes in this field at Buck's Nook, Gateshead, indicate the location of the ditch of an Iron Age farmstead. The soil in the filled-in ditches allows the crop to grow more quickly and ripen later than the crops over the surrounding soil. They appear as differently coloured bands from above. These are known as cropmarks and many sites are known only from cropmarks spotted on aerial photographs.

IMAGINARY CELTS

Some history books tell you that the Ancient Britons were an Iron Age Celtic people, the ancestors of the Scottish, Irish and Welsh speakers of the Gaelic languages. But the term Celtic is rather misleading. The people called the Keltoi by the Greeks and the Celtae by the Romans lived in southern France and northern Spain. Roman writers had a different word for the people of the British Isles – they were called Prittani. In fact, the term 'Celtic' was only applied to indigenous people of the British Isles in the early 18th century. There is no evidence in modern excavations or in genetic research that these islands were settled by Celts in the early Iron Age. The real ancestry of the Iron Age inhabitants of the British Isles lies deep in the very earliest settlement of what became Eastern England, following the retreat of the ice sheets at the end of the last Ice Age.

We do however get a glimpse of the religious beliefs of the Ancient Britons in the form of Roman period stone sculptures of the heads of gods or warriors. Romans simply accepted the gods of the local people alongside their own gods and the deified emperors.

Ancient Celts, with tattoos, as depicted in Eneas MacKenzie's View of the County of Northumberland, 1825. The Prittani (like the Picts) were said to have tattoos.

These stone heads from local sites are of Roman date but are probably of local, Iron Age gods. They can be seen in the Great North Museum.

RETURN TO THE RIVER

Whatever name we give to the pre-Roman North Easterners, there is little trace of their earthly remains. Of over two dozen Iron Age homesteads excavated between the Tees and the Tyne, the only human remains recorded are two loose teeth found at Thorpe Thewles near Stockton. A skull unearthed in a garden at Marden, North Tyneside, may have belonged to a nearby farmstead of the Iron Age, but may equally date from Roman times. The practice of excarnation that was used in the preceding millennia probably continued, but rather than being sealed in barrows, the remaining bones may well have been burnt on funeral pyres, well away from the villages and farms of the population. Another possibility is that the dead were placed in the river, like the bronze swords and spears dredged from the Tyne.

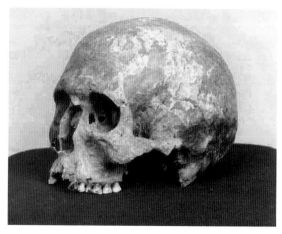

This skull was found near an Iron Age site at Marden, North Tyneside.

Whatever the detail of the ceremonies involved, there is an almost complete absence of burial sites dating to this period – the 700 years before the Roman Conquest in AD 71. If any such sites existed, it is likely that they would have been encountered, either accidentally during building work or during one of the nearly 300 excavations to have taken place in Tyne & Wear over the past 100 years

Also dating to the Iron Age, and often coming to light when the river banks were developed for Victorian industry, are a group of dug-out canoes. Made from a solid tree trunk, hollowed out by a combination of fire scorching and chiselling, they are usually discovered where a side stream joins a larger river.

TWAM

An Iron Age dug-out canoe from County Durham – The Westgate Road canoe would have appeared very similar to this canoe, which was found in a river bank at Cartington, County Durham.

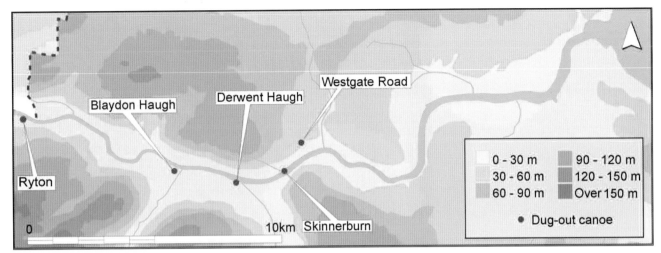

This map identifies the places on the Tyne where canoes have been found.

One such canoe was unearthed at the very bottom of Westgate Road near the Black Gate. It is too small to have been practical, and was buried in a channel that would have been too small to navigate, at the top of the bank overlooking the Tyne.

As with the metalwork that has been recovered from the river, there may have been a religious aspect to the burial of such a vessel. Perhaps it contained a body that was being sent on its way to the afterlife.

This photograph is all that remains of this Iron Age dug-out canoe, which was found in Gateshead in 1912. These wooden canoes only survived due to the wet conditions in which they were buried and often perish when exposed to the air.

19

This massive carving is the tombstone of a Roman cavalryman named Flavinus, who was stationed at Corstopitum (Corbridge). The inscription tells us that he died aged twenty-five, between the years AD 79 and AD 98, after serving for seven years, but the relief implies that he slaughtered plenty of the local barbarians before he died. The figure being trampled is a local warrior, shown as naked and shaggy-haired with an inferior local sword, a pathetic creature compared to the glorious soldier of the Roman army. From finds of pins, brooches and fastenings, we can be quite certain that the natives of northern England did wear clothes, making this a piece of propaganda which depicts the enemies of the Roman as savages.

The stone is preserved at Hexham Abbey.

THE EAGLE GOES NORTH

The landscape encountered by the Roman Army was similar to that of today, with most of the countryside being open fields and pasture, divided by belts of wild woodland and uncultivated scrub and heath, and featuring large patches of marshland and bog. In north-east England the people of the Iron Age lived in scattered villages, grouped into loose clans or tribes linked by common ancestors and shared customs, but without strong leaders with control over large areas. This raised a problem for the Roman generals planning the conquest and occupation of the north. In southern England, the local hillforts and tribal capitals became the sites of the forts of the Roman legions. Compliant Iron Age kings would be supported and protected by the legionaries, while any sign of resistance would be ruthlessly crushed. In the absence of any tribal power centres in coastal north-east England, the Roman military placed the forts of the occupation forces at strategic locations in the communications system, the river crossings and major route ways, and at religious sites, to impose their authority upon the scattered local population.

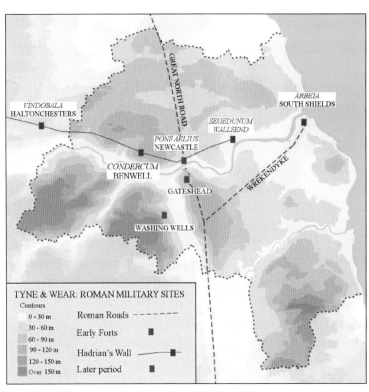

TYNE & WEAR: ROMAN MILITARY SITES

Contours
0 - 30 m
30 - 60 m
60 - 90 m
90 - 120 m
120 - 150 m
Over 150 m

Roman Roads - - - - -

Early Forts ■

Hadrian's Wall ——■

Later period ■

ON THE WAY TO SCOTLAND

By AD 83, the Roman army had swept through the north of Britain in the drive to conquer the whole island, culminating with the slaughter of 10,000 hostile tribesmen at the Battle of Mons Graupius in Northern Scotland. However, they found that although they would often defeat the Scottish tribes they could not subdue them, or hold down their territory. The effort of conquering the Scots would have been far greater than the rewards.

While they pushed northwards, the army left the Tyne area with only light defences in the hands of small numbers of troops. Excavations suggest that there were late 1st century AD forts at Corstopitum (Corbridge) and Arbeia (South Shields). At Newcastle, excavations on the high ground overlooking the river have revealed tantalising glimpses of Roman activity. Between 1977 and 1992 a programme of digging in the Castle Garth revealed evidence of ploughing, which may date to the first Roman occupation of Newcastle, and coins and other finds from the time of the first Roman rulers of the local population.

The outline of a Roman fort at Washingwell.

ROMANS ON BOTTLE BANK

The most important archaeological discovery in Gateshead in the last hundred years is the Roman village on Bottle Bank. Before 1994 no reliable Roman finds had been recovered from the south bank, but excavations on Bottle Bank in advance of the construction of the Gateshead Hilton hotel located a Roman settlement dating back to the 2nd century AD and enduring until the 4th.

When new buildings are proposed in those parts of Tyneside where archaeology might be found, the law states that the developer must investigate the site before construction work begins. In this way, the most important remains can be discovered and excavated properly.

Excavations over a wide area give a better picture of a neighbourhood than a few trenches can. By excavating the houses of the settlement like this, we see how buildings relate to each other and how the land was divided up

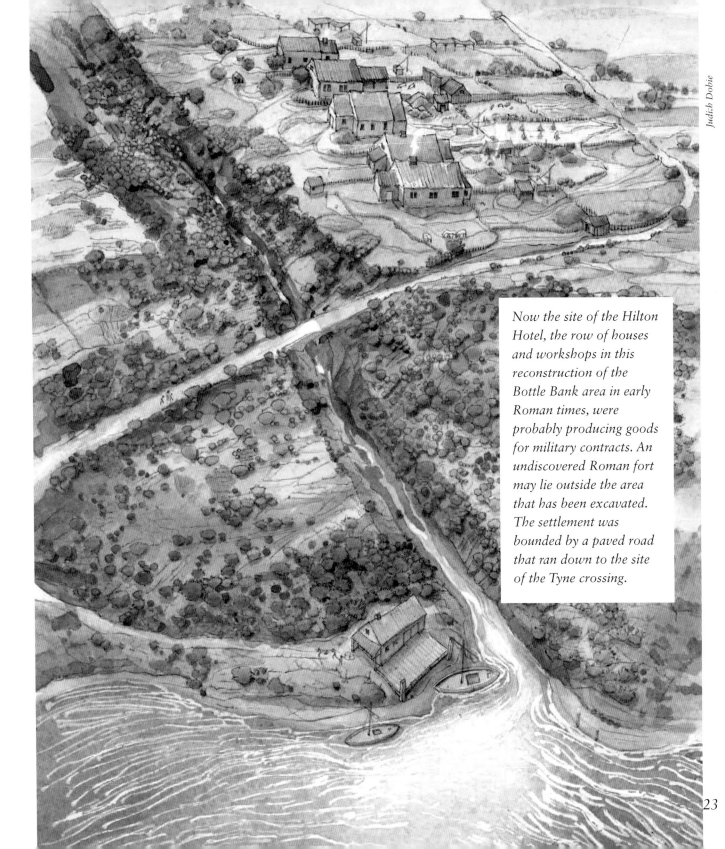

Now the site of the Hilton Hotel, the row of houses and workshops in this reconstruction of the Bottle Bank area in early Roman times, were probably producing goods for military contracts. An undiscovered Roman fort may lie outside the area that has been excavated. The settlement was bounded by a paved road that ran down to the site of the Tyne crossing.

Ditches divided the area into small plots with buildings. In the small area available for excavation, one building was a wooden house later rebuilt in stone. This small settlement sat by a road leading to the river bank and probably represents the growth of a settlement to take advantage of the trade on the Roman road, perhaps a generation before the construction of the bridge and the fort on the northern shore.

Each property had an area for industrial activity, a hearth, and a proper water supply. A Roman well was located near the houses, close to the present day High Street, and the individual back yards of the houses had water cisterns to provide water for animals and for industrial use.

Courtesy Oxford Archaeology North

The water cisterns were lined with stone to stop clay discolouring the water.

This Roman well on Bottle Bank was excavated by machine. Modern safety rules prohibit digging by hand within the shaft. There were almost no finds at the bottom, not even the usual rusty bucket!

Behind the plots, a paved road, right, marked the edge of the settlement and ran down the slope towards the site of the bridge. It was well made with flagged slabs covering a simple drain. It was built in the 3rd century when the settlement was flourishing and at least one timber house was re-built in stone.

The inhabitants used pottery from the same markets as the Roman Army. The storage pot shown below in its original position, was made in Kent. Nothing survived of its contents.

By AD 270, however, the settlement was in decline and soon abandoned. There was no evidence here of life in the late Roman period. For that we must look north of the river.

Courtesy Oxford Archaeology North

Part of the paved Roman road that runs round the settlement. Flagstones would have covered the whole drain.

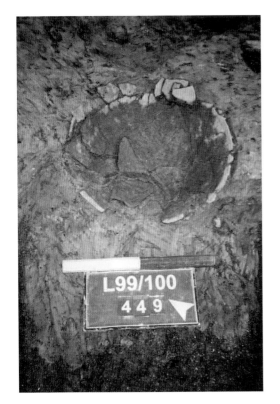

Like many of the Roman deposits on the Bottle Bank site, this shell-tempered pot from North Kent (left) was partly destroyed by gardening and the digging of rubbish and cess pits in the Middle Ages.

ACKNOWLEDGING THE GODS

Numerous Roman altars and statuary were dredged from the river crossing and excavated from the surrounding area in the 19th century. Altars take the form of short pillars with a flat area on the top where sacrifices could be made. The deities honoured include Jupiter, Saturn, Mercury, Neptune, Oceanus and 'the Mother Goddesses of my homeland'. Altars were commissioned by individuals or military units. Some altars may have been in small shrines, along with carvings of gods such as the figures of Fortuna or Mercury, shown here, and placed in the best room of the house. These carvings were found near Newcastle, and can be seen in the Great North Museum.

Fortuna, the goddess of good luck and fate, is carrying a horn of plenty and a ship's rudder (for steering the fates). Cults of Fortuna are found throughout the Roman Empire.

Mercury was popular in Britain and Gaul said Julius Caesar. He is the messenger of the gods, guide of the dead, and protector of merchants, shepherds, gamblers, liars and thieves. He is often shown with his 'caduceus' in his left hand. This short staff is entwined by two serpents, a symbol of commerce or negotiation.

This Roman altar base was unearthed at Bottle Bank and is seen here in the finds hut, shortly after excavation.

Above, an altar to Oceanus from the Tyne at the site of the Roman crossing of Pons Aelius. Oceanus was the god of Okeanos, the great river said to encircle the world and was sacred to rivers, wells and springs. This altar was placed there by the victorious Sixth Legion.

Left, this altar is from the temple to a little-known god, Antenociticus, excavated near the Wall at Benwell.

HADRIAN'S WALL

His inspections of the northern frontier in AD 121 led the Emperor Hadrian to question the wisdom of conquering Scotland. He then decided to define the northern limit of the Roman Empire with a strong boundary wall. At the time, a string of small forts had loosely marked the frontier between the Solway Firth and Corbridge, certainly, and possibly extending to South Shields at the mouth of the Tyne. Wanting to improve this frontier, Hadrian commanded his army to build a wall to run from coast to coast. A seasoned army officer who was interested in architecture and built his own palace in Rome, Hadrian is thought to have designed the Wall himself. It was built on high ground, using stone on the eastern sections and turf in the west. It was a 5m-high barrier to the barbarians beyond, studded with small forts called milecastles at every Roman mile, each with a gateway allowing civilian traffic through the frontier, but forming a massive physical and psychological barrier to enemies of Rome.

The path of the Wall is very evident at Denton, just west of Newcastle, where the West Road follows a fairly straight line from the city centre. A section of the Wall can be seen on the right.

DEFENDING THE EMPIRE

Hadrian's Wall was strengthened by several other defensive features. A deep ditch ran along the front of the Wall to prevent the approach of attackers. The small area between the ditch and the Wall is known as the berm and was filled with a dense entanglement of sharpened branches set in rows of oval-shaped pits. These were called 'cippi' pits by the Romans and are described by the Roman General Julius Caesar in his account of the Gallic Wars. They provided extra protection to the stone Wall. About 20m behind the Wall was the Military Way, a supply road that linked the forts, (every five Roman miles) the milecastles (every Roman mile) and the intermediate turrets (one third of a Roman mile). 80m behind the road was the Vallum, a ditch between two earth banks, an extra frontier obstacle that helped control traffic through set checkpoints along the frontier.

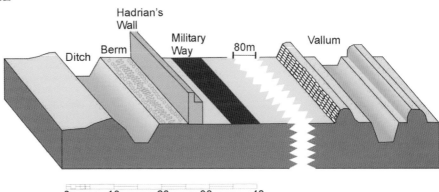

These cippi pits are being excavated beside a stretch of the Wall at Shields Road, Byker.

'... *These stakes being sunk into this trench, and fastened firmly at the bottom, to prevent the possibility of their being torn up, had their branches only projecting from the ground. There were five rows ... whoever entered within them were likely to impale themselves on very sharp stakes. The soldiers called these cippi.' (Julius Caesar: The Gallic Wars, LXXII – LXXIII.)*

THE WALL TO THE EAST OF THE CITY: SHIELDS ROAD, BYKER

Some of these features were located when the Wall was uncovered in Shields Road, Byker, in 2000. As far back as 1725 the Wall had been recorded by the antiquarian William Stukeley, but the exact line along the modern street was lost until it was rediscovered directly below the Victorian shops opposite Byker Pool. Only the foundation course of the Wall survived but, in the photographs below, the cippi pits can be seen very clearly after excavation between the Wall foundations on the left and the dark soil of the filled-in defensive ditch. As the ditch ran under the modern pavement it was not possible to excavate the contents of the ditch.

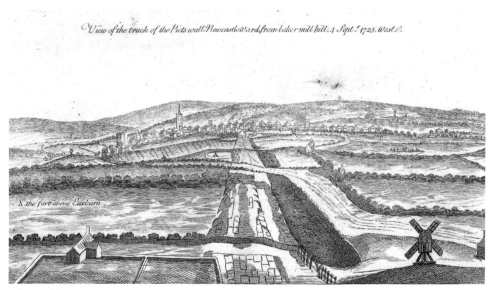

The Wall is clearly depicted by William Stukeley in this drawing.

The Wall foundations were 8ft wide but only 6 inches deep.

The rows of cippi pits are clearly visible to the right of the Wall foundations.

THE WALL IN THE CITY: JOINING THE DOTS

Where the Wall runs through open countryside it is easy to trace the route of the still exposed remains, but in the city centre the Wall has largely vanished under 900 years of dense occupation. Numerous excavations over the last two centuries have hit upon fragments of its foundations or come across the ditch that ran in front of the Wall. We must join the dots between excavations to sketch out its location and still there are stretches where we have lost its course entirely.

In 2003, a 13m stretch of the Wall's base was found under the concrete floor of a 1960s garage at the corner of Melbourne Street and Gibson Street, indicating that portions of the Wall have survived undiscovered beneath modern buildings. A new hotel was built on the derelict site, with foundation beams that spanned across the remains of the Roman Wall, which was preserved, undamaged.

The remains of the Roman Wall run through the foundations of the 1960s garage.

The Wall is revealed beneath the foundations of a Victorian warehouse at Garth Heads, City Road.

In the centre of Newcastle the course of the Wall was revealed immediately under the concrete surface of a yard at Garth Heads, City Road. Again, though the above-ground walling had been robbed and re-used, the foundations survived.

We are unsure of the line of the Roman frontier across the oldest part of the city, but the path of the Wall was also discovered during building work at Cooper's Auction Mart at the bottom of Westgate Road. Finding the Wall meant that the building could not be demolished as the City Council will not allow the Wall, which is now a World Heritage Site, to be damaged during redevelopment.

TWAM

Courtesy Tim Crocker / Ryder Architecture

Cooper's Auction Mart was renovated and the Wall left undisturbed.

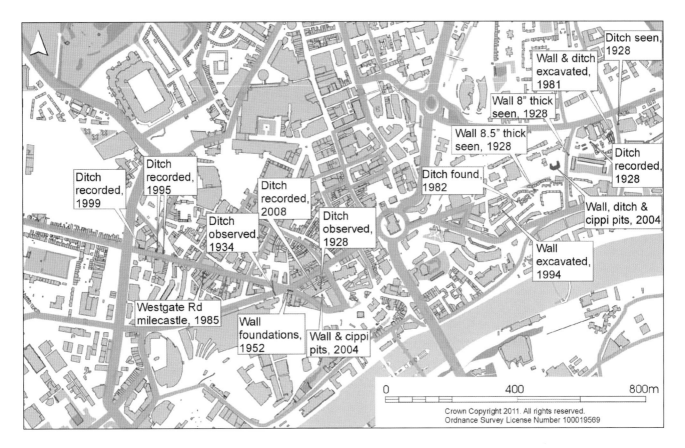

Ditch seen, 1928

Wall & ditch excavated, 1981

Wall 8" thick seen, 1928

Wall 8.5" thick seen, 1928

Ditch recorded, 1995

Ditch recorded, 1999

Ditch recorded, 2008

Ditch observed, 1934

Ditch observed, 1928

Ditch found, 1982

Ditch recorded, 1928

Wall, ditch & cippi pits, 2004

Wall excavated, 1994

Westgate Rd milecastle, 1985

Wall foundations, 1952

Wall & cippi pits, 2004

0   400   800m

Crown Copyright 2011. All rights reserved.
Ordnance Survey License Number 100019569

This map shows the locations of the excavations which have uncovered evidence of the Wall under the city. It is easy to trace the eastern and western sections but the location of the central portion is still a mystery. There have been numerous excavations in this area, some in the predicted paths of the Wall, but no sign has been found so far.

Right, looking for the Roman Wall on the West Road, 2010.

MILECASTLES AND TURRETS

The spacings of the milecastles and turrets on the Wall were worked out by the Durham archaeologist, Sir Ian Richmond, in 1930, counting westwards from Wallsend (Segedunum). It was a real surprise, therefore, when a new milecastle was discovered 'in the wrong place' at Black Swan Yard on Westgate Road, on a small dig when Newcastle Arts Centre was being renovated in the 1980s.

A small section of the foundations of the Westgate Road Milecastle, with part of the south gateway, was found in 1985 by local potter David Fry. The position of the south wall shows that the front wall was under the pavement of Westgate Road.

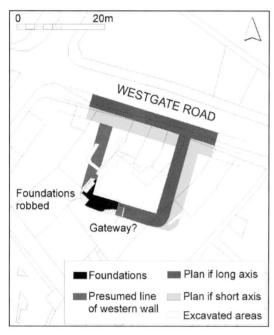

The plan above shows the position of the unexpected milecastle on Westgate Road. There were two types of milecastle, one with a short axis, one with a long axis. Either might have been the type here. We are unable to tell as the front wall is beneath the pavement.

A good example of a turret is on display on the West Road at Denton, above. The turrets were strongpoints between milecastles which provided shelter and viewing platforms for the soldiers manning the Wall.

Foundations of the Roman milecastle in Westgate Road can be seen in Black Swan Yard. In 2011, as part of the wider renovation of historic buildings on Westgate Road, a new plaque was unveiled by the Leader of Newcastle City Council, Councillor Nick Forbes, to celebrate the Roman heritage of this part of the city. Mike Tilley of Newcastle Arts Centre described the discovery.

WESTGATE ROAD

A HADRIAN'S WALL MILECASTLE
2nd century A.D.

In 1985 the south west corner of a milecastle (fortified gate) was discovered here. It formed part of the Roman frontier fortifications of Hadrian's Wall.

CITY OF NEWCASTLE UPON TYNE

Steve Brock

Steve Brock

PONS AELIUS: THE BRIDGE AT NEWCASTLE

The Roman bridge lay on a road leading north from Chester-le-Street but its exact position is unknown.

The fort and settlement took their name from the Pons Aelius, or the Bridge of the Aelia, the family of the Emperors Hadrian and Antoninus Pius, builder of the Antonine Wall further to the north. Only one other bridge in the entire Roman Empire bore this name and that crossed the Tiber in Rome itself. The name shows the importance of the river crossing and the tight tie between the bridge and the Wall. There may well have been a large ceremonial monument on the approach to the bridge, possibly a triumphal arch or a heroic statue of the Emperor Hadrian, to mark the original starting point of the Wall, but this would be in an area now covered by thousands of tons of later river ballast dumping and quayside reclamation.

This altar to Neptune, god of water, rivers and the sea, along with an altar to Oceanus were found in the Tyne in the 19th century. They came from a shrine on the bridge. The Romans were superstitious travellers who made offerings before setting out on long journeys.

Newcastle artist John Storey drew this impression of the Roman Bridge at Pons Aelius for John Collingwood Bruce's The Roman Wall (second edition, 1853).

SMOKE AND MIRRORS

At its height the Roman Empire spanned three continents and had many thousands of kilometres of borders and frontiers to construct, maintain and man. Hadrian's Wall alone was made up of sixteen major forts, many minor forts, eighty milecastles and 111km of walling. It would have taken a huge number of soldiers to patrol and defend these boundaries. The Roman letters found at the fort of Vindolanda suggest that it was common practice for squads of soldiers to move frequently between the various milecastles and forts. The Wall and its forts were part of a 'smoke and mirrors' plan by the Roman army to trick the enemy into thinking the frontier garrison was larger than it was. Within the high walls of each fort the true number of soldiers present was concealed from prying eyes. Once the impressive and intimidating monument had been built, the army simply needed to make it look lived in.

In 1903, this stone was dredged out of the Tyne near the Swing Bridge. From the inscription we know that this is an imperial dedication slab. It was set up in honour of the Emperor Antoninus Pius by several legions serving in the area. We can date this very closely, to between AD 155 and AD 159, because it mentions that Julius Verus was governor of Britain and we know from other records that he held office for those four years.

THE VICTORIOUS LEGIONS

Scattered across the city and the banks and bed of the river are the finds of Roman altars already mentioned. These stones were not the work of priests seeking to convert the natives – they were tokens of gratitude from the soldiers who had been brought from their homelands in the Provinces of the Roman Empire to the wet and hilly outskirts of the known world and had survived. As legions and as individuals, they raised altars to the gods they felt had blessed them and to the memory of their leaders and their own achievements. The First Cohort of Ulpian Cugerni, natives of Germany, proudly called themselves citizens of Rome, their newly awarded title (The Emperor Caracalla opened citizenship rights to far more people in AD 212) and honoured the emperor's mother, Julia Domna, at the fort at Newcastle. The Victorious Sixth Legion pronounced themselves loyal and faithful and gave thanks to the sea gods by placing altars on the new bridge over the Tyne. In these inscriptions we can see the pride and solidarity of the invading army, some of Italian birth, but most descended from other conquered barbarians who were now proud to be part of the Roman Empire.

THE ROMAN FORT

The Romans were here for a long time and numerous large forts were built into the Wall itself, including Segedunum (Wallsend), Housesteads and Vindolanda (a little to the south of the Wall). These forts were designed as a part of the vast and intimidating Roman military machine. Excavations in the 1970s proved that the fort at Newcastle was not one of the original wall forts. Instead it sat a little to the south of the Wall, on the same hilltop now occupied by the medieval castle. The fort was built in the late 2nd or early 3rd century, up to ninety years after the beginning of the Wall's construction. Current thinking is that the fort was built during the campaign of Emperor Septimus Severus to punish hostile Scottish tribes in the early 200s AD. To support his army, Severus rebuilt many forts along the main Roman roads and ordered the construction of new facilities such as the granaries at South Shields. The quick movement of troops, supplies and intelligence was an important part of the success of the Roman army.

A stone Mercury from the Roman fort.

Only ten per cent of the fort at Newcastle was excavated but from this we can tell that it had a regular layout, adjusted to fit onto the space available on the promontory, that it had a cross-shaped street plan found in many of the forts of Severus, and that it was relatively small. As the Roman army built its forts to a standard design across the Empire, it is possible to make guesses to fill in the gaps between the excavated remains.

TWAM

This crucible for working bronze was another find from the Roman fort.

There was however one very non-standard item which has drawn more guesses than any other aspect of the fort. During the late 3rd century, a bronze dodecahedron (a shape with twelve identical sides) was placed on a small platform inside the east granary of the Roman fort, possibly as part of a ceremony of dedication. We have no idea what it was for or why it was important that it be placed there. Similar items were also found at South Shields and Corbridge Roman fort, as well as nine other British sites. People have suggested that they were used as surveying instruments, candlesticks or dice. The most recent suggestion is that the dodecahedrons are ceremonial mace heads, used in religious rituals. Until further discoveries are made, we are left with a beautiful object and an intriguing mystery.

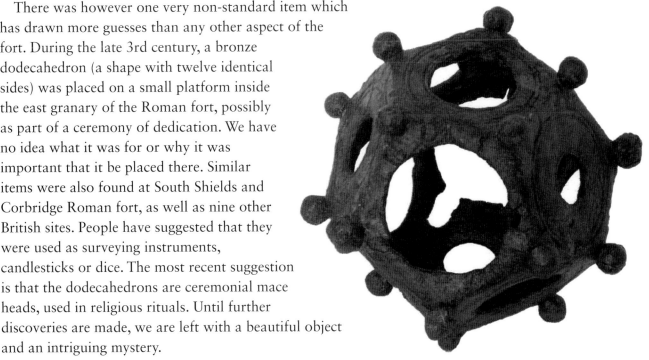

This mystery object from the Roman fort is on display at the Keep.

This beautiful Roman 'trumpet brooch' is made of a copper alloy which has turned green over time and was decorated with blue enamel which survives in places. The pin is missing but it is otherwise complete. Similar trumpet brooches have been found in the North East, in 1st or 2nd century sites. It is on display at the Keep.

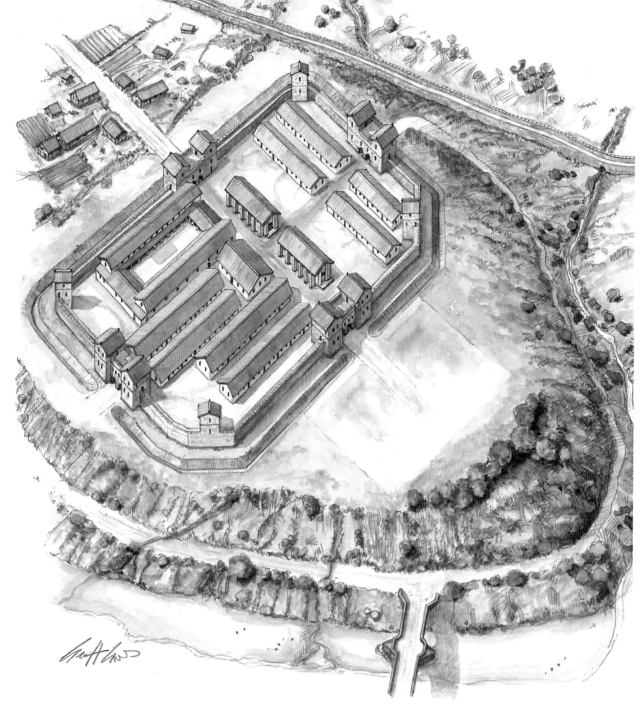

Geoff Laws

This artistic reconstruction shows the fort as it may have looked around AD 250. There are steep slopes on three sides, and the West Gate, top left, was probably the main gate into the fort from the civilian settlement, the vicus. Hadrian's Wall lies to the north of the fort running along the line of the present day street called Side.

AND THE CIVILIANS

It is easy to be overwhelmed by all the forts, roads and the size of the Wall and imagine the Roman North as a warzone, empty of everyone except constantly patrolling legionaries and wild barbarians. In fact, there is little sign that the Wall saw much actual combat and none that the fort in Newcastle was ever attacked. At Newcastle, as at other forts along the frontier, there is evidence for the civilian population who lived in the settlements that grew up around the fort. Everyday life on the Roman frontier is known to us from finds such as pottery, building foundations and cobbled roads. Most Roman forts had an associated civilian settlement just outside their gates, called a vicus. A garrison would require supplies and services, drawing people to set up shop nearby in order to meet the demand.

This is part of a bone comb once used in the Roman fort. As in some modern combs, the teeth on one side are more widely spaced than on the other, an arrangement that was popular with both the Romans and the Anglo-Saxons. The iron rivet held the two sides of the comb together.

PAX ROMANA

The population of the vicus was dependent on the fort for trade and income, and might rise and fall along with the number of soldiers stationed there. During busy periods, such as major dates in the military religious calendar, the vicus might fill up with opportunistic traders, as with the stalls that spring up around major events today. Away from the Imperial Frontier, most of the native population continued to live their lives in the wider countryside, farming the land in the

same way they had been doing for generations before the arrival of the Romans.

Most shopping was done at markets, where the craftsmen of the vicus and the local farmers would set up stalls to sell their wares, either in exchange for items they needed or for Roman coins. The Roman era was the first period in which coins were used in Britain and their presence is extremely useful for archaeologists. On sites from the Roman period onwards, they are one of the

This bronze jug was found in Newcastle.

TWAM

best indicators of the date of the buildings being excavated. However, allowance must be made for old coins continuing in circulation. For instance, several Roman coins issued by emperors who reigned before the Roman army arrived in the area have been dredged out of the Tyne.

This coin (both sides are shown) is from the reign of the Emperor Hadrian.

Due to their temporary nature, marketplaces can be hard to identify through archaeology, but there are hints of the vicus marketplace which must have existed at Newcastle. Cobbled areas and remains of buildings have been found at the bottom of Westgate Road, near St Nicholas Buildings, which might have been part of a market outside the west gate of the fort. A find of a large number of late Roman low-value coins in the open space at the centre of the fort suggests that by about AD 300, after the vicus was abandoned, the marketplace moved inside the fort and its location is marked by the lost small change of the shoppers.

The Roman frontier was an exotic melting pot, teeming with local as well as foreign traders, craftsmen and opportunists.

Crafts and small industries like iron forging and bronze working were mixed among the shops and houses of the streets. Taverns and brothels would welcome both the local soldiers and passing trade. Larger settlements would have a bath-house, which both civilians and soldiers would have used.

BREAD AND TRADE

In Roman society the type of bread eaten was an important indicator of status. White bread wheat was eaten by the Roman rulers, while the local population ate the Spelt wheat, which makes a hard, black bread. Soldiers were partly paid in grain to make flour for bread.

The Roman army needed large numbers of small, light, hand-millstones for the soldiers, who were partly paid in grain. The left hand example is of local sandstone, the other is a German basalt quern from the Rhineland. Both were found in the fort at Newcastle.

LAYERS UPON LAYERS

The Roman fort continued in use over several centuries. Many buildings were demolished and rebuilt during its lifespan. At first glance it can be difficult for the archaeologists to tell which remains belong to each period.

In sites like these, the 'stratigraphy' is particularly important. The lowest layer on any site is the natural ground surface, before any human activity took place. On top of this is the first occupation layer, made up of rubbish, building remains, and accumulated soil left by the first human occupants. More occupation layers build up on top of that.

Excavations must dig down through these layers, stopping at the natural surface. From this backwards view, archaeologists must then work out the proper order of events.

This map shows the distribution of late Roman coins found in the centre of the of the fort, which suggests that after the vicus was abandoned the market moved inside the fort.

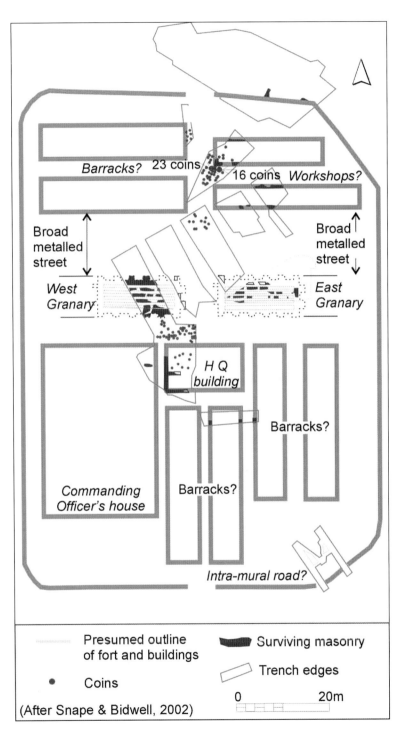

Barracks? 23 coins

16 coins *Workshops?*

Broad metalled street

Broad metalled street

West Granary

East Granary

H Q building

Barracks?

Commanding Officer's house

Barracks?

Intra-mural road?

---- Presumed outline of fort and buildings

• Coins

◣ Surviving masonry

▱ Trench edges

0   20m

(After Snape & Bidwell, 2002)

DAUGHTERS OF EMPIRE

In 1903, workmen at Clavering Place stumbled over two Roman stone coffins, containing human bone and charcoal. The Romans used the same Greek word for stone coffins as we use – sarcophagus – which means 'flesh–eater'. In 2009, when a neighbouring site was redeveloped, it was not a complete surprise when two more coffins were found, one of them still sealed with steel pins hammered into lead plugs in the lid of the coffin. This discovery generated a great deal of interest and there was a large media presence for the opening of one of the coffins in July 2009. Any hopes of spectacular finds were shattered by the very poor preservation of the remains.

There was just enough bone to show that one of the coffins contained a baby and a young girl, while the other contained the remains of a young woman. All that survived in the way of personal ornaments was a finely made pin of Whitby jet and a string of tiny glass beads.

These imposing coffins were expensive and available only to the wealthiest families that lived in the area. The exquisitely carved pin would have been used to hold in place a fashionable Roman hairstyle, imitating the Roman empresses such as Julia Domna, who began a trend for a large roll of hair pinned to the back of the head while tresses fell forward to frame the face. These girls, wearing Roman clothing and buried in expensive stone coffins, probably belonged to the family of the garrison commander, who was always a high-ranking professional soldier of the Roman upper class.

The coffins discovered at Clavering Place in 2009.

TWAM

Above, a coffin uncovered at Clavering Place in 1903. The interior is so small that it is believed to be for a child. It contained a pottery beaker, human bone and charcoal.

The decorated vase was inside the other coffin, where it was being used as an urn. Pottery is divided up into many types, known as 'wares', based on where and how they were made – this beaker is Caster Ware. This ware was made in the Nene Valley from the mid-2nd century and was an ornate brand considered the equal of imported pottery.

The opening of the coffin, July 2009, and right, the skeletal outline of the coffin's occupant.

The fine Whitby jet pin and some blue glass beads, below left, were the only belongings that survived in the coffin.

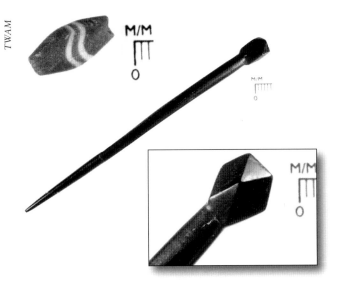

It must have seemed a cruel irony to a successful career soldier that he survived battles while his daughters did not reach adulthood and were left buried by a road near a small fort on the outer fringes of the Empire.

THE VICUS AT PONS AELIUS

Alerted by the discovery of the coffins, a major excavation was undertaken at Clavering Place in the summer of 2009. It has given us our best glimpse of the Roman vicus at Pons Aelius. As at Bottle Bank, a series of tenements were laid beside a Roman road, with houses and shops made of timber, some with stone foundations. Such dwellings are known as strip houses because they tend to be arranged in long thin rows. As at Gateshead, the settlement did not develop into a significant Roman town, and the remains in the ground were insubstantial.

The road ran from the west gate of the fort, 200m to the north-east, to the steep slope that led towards the bridge across the river. It had a paved surface, sloped on either side to allow rain water to drain into ditches.

A general view of the excavations at Clavering Place.

The Roman metalled road emerges from the excavation. The surface is cut by medieval rubbish pits.

Among the finds was a red-burnished bowl of a Gaulish type known as 'Samian', used as a container for a small cremation burial. This may pre-date the construction of the strip houses.

A large hand-mill of German basalt was found in a pit in one of the rear yards. The inhabitants of the vicus had access to 'Romanised' goods and the newly fashionable lifestyle and eating habits found across the Empire. We don't know if the owner of the basalt mill was the dependant of a Roman auxilliary soldier or a native trader or craftsman.

Courtesy Archaeological Services Durham University

Top, the excavation of the Samian cremation.

Above, the basalt handmill is painstakingly removed.

Left, recording Roman period rubbish pits containing pottery and bone.

BENWELL'S OWN GOD: ANTENOCITICUS

The fort at Newcastle was part of a long string of forts near the Wall. To the east was the Wallsend fort of Segedunum, to the west the Benwell fort. Nothing is visible of the fort of Condercum at Benwell itself as it is sliced through by the Newcastle-Carlisle road, while houses and a reservoir have destroyed much beneath the surface. However, about 50m to the east of the fort is the Temple of Antenociticus. Its foundations, along with casts of its altars, are visible on Broomridge Avenue and can be visited. The temple was discovered in 1862, complete with several altars and fragments of the cult statue.

Both the temple and the cult of Antenociticus were small – the temple is less than 10m in length and contains the only written references to this god in all of the Roman empire. The Romans worshipped a great many gods, from famous deities like Jupiter or Minerva whose worship spanned the empire, down to the little gods of individual springs such as Coventina whose well can be found just along the Wall at Carrawburgh.

Antenociticus was one of the little gods. When the Romans encountered

Above, a tinted postcard shows how the temple looked in the late 19th century.

Below, the temple is now in the care of English Heritage and can be visited in Broomridge Avenue, just off the West Road.

a new god, they simply added it to their pantheon or equated it with an existing god. It is thought that Antenociticus was either a local god or the patron deity of one of the cohorts posted at Benwell.

From the burnt timbers and roof tiles that have been excavated, we can tell that the temple was destroyed by fire in the late 2nd century. Most likely the cult of Antenociticus ended with his only temple.

The inscriptions on the two altars state that both were set up by a soldier who 'willingly and deservedly fulfilled his vow'. Worshippers of the Roman gods often promised to set up an altar to a deity if that deity aided them in some way. Evidently this soldier felt that Antenociticus had kept his side of the bargain and was now fulfilling his. One altar and part of the other were found in 1862. The rest of the second altar was eventually uncovered in 1904, built into the foundations of a nearby house.

Such small temples were a feature of every Roman military site. A reconstruction can be seen at Vindolanda.

This statue was once at the heart of the Temple of Antenociticus – a life-sized image of the god watching over the altars and rituals in his honour. The style of the statue is an interesting meeting of Roman and native art, incorporating features from both traditions. Only this head and parts of the limbs have been found.

ROMAN TYNESIDE, AD 200

This scene shows a reconstruction of the Roman fort and its surroundings at the beginning of the 3rd century. The river is much broader than it is today and still has its natural banks, as the straight banks we see today were created in the 13th century.

The Roman bridge, Pons Aelius, spans the river and links the fort on the northern bank to the settlement at Bottle Bank.

The vicus sprawls out to the north-west of the fort, following the military road parallel to Hadrian's Wall.

To the east of the fort, the Wall crossed the Lort Burn and follows a path set back from the riverbank to avoid the steep marshy ground at the mouth of Pandon Burn.

Between the two tributaries, a milecastle guards the point where the Great North Road passes through the wall, following its ancient route despite the Roman building work.

This landscape shaped the development of the city – today the Great North Road is Pilgrim Street, the fort lies beneath the castle and Westgate Road follows the line of the Wall.

The fort is where the Castle Keep now stands, and much of the vicus is covered by Newcastle Central Station.

Judith Dobie

THE ROMAN RETREAT: WHAT NEXT?

During the 4th century the military presence in the north of England was reduced, and forts that once held 600 troops now housed only 200 or 150. But the gradual reduction and then disappearance of Roman Imperial authority does not necessarily mean the abandonment of a military presence. Instead, the garrisons in the forts were used by a native army kept active by the external threat from hostile tribes during a period of great upheaval and uncertainty. In northern England many of the soldiers, like the Cugerni at Newcastle or the Frisians at Rudchester, originally came from what is now modern Germany, northern France and the Low Countries, giving contemporary society a distinctly Germanic character.

The accepted history of England, written many years later by historians such as Bede, assumes that warlike Angles and Saxons invaded, replacing the native Britons or driving them westwards, where their descendents would become the Gaelic-speaking peoples of Wales and South-West England. The Germanic invaders eventually settled in the conquered land, making England their own.

However recent studies into the genetics of the people of the British Isles suggest that only perhaps five per cent of the modern gene pool derived from Germanic populations, with the vast majority made up of descendents of the first settlers of early prehistory. The archaeological evidence suggests that the everyday artefacts and buildings in England at this time are increasingly similar to those found on the continent. This gradual change could just as well have come about through increased contact and trade rather than invasion. As we saw in prehistory, there was always a certain amount of contact across the North Sea and the English Channel, enough to establish distant but powerful kinship links.

TWAM

We now have an alternative to the traditional story: when the Roman army left, many Germanic and Gallic auxilliary soldiers stayed behind with their British wives and families as part of a new local army supporting the local ruling class, as happened across the Continent when the tide of Roman power finally ebbed. A new society, which is a complex fusion of many strands, develops into new social groups, partly based on the

This bronze brooch was found just outside the Roman fort at Benwell. It dates to the 7th century, long after the fort was officially abandoned. It is a valuable item decorated in a Germanic style. Perhaps it was a possession of a member of a warband and may have been placed in a grave which was disturbed by later building.

Roman military, and partly on a local re-emergence of pre-Roman culture. There is a more Continental, Germanic, feel to the lifestyle, but the genetic pool is largely unchanged.

RISE OF THE WARBANDS

Early written sources talk of 'warbands' of local warriors who ruled over the farmers that made up most of the population. These warbands may have been the descendents of the Roman garrison, protecting the local population but drawing supplies directly from the surrounding countryside, rather than from the Roman Army. At Birdoswald, a fort at the west end of the Wall, remains of wooden buildings in the local style were found on top of the remains of the fort's buildings, which shows that people continued to live in the fort and build new buildings within it. At the same time, one of the granaries seems to have been converted into a hall. The ex-soldiers and their

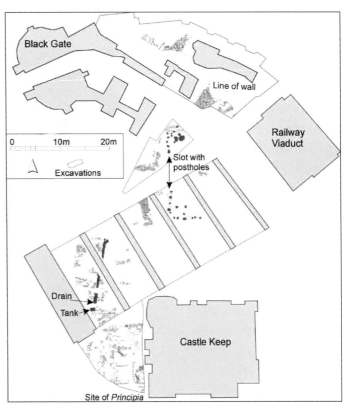

This plan shows how excavated postholes revealed where timber structures were built over the Roman fort on the site of the Castle Keep. (After Nolan and Harbottle, 2010.)

descendents seem to have continued to occupy the fort as the military arm of the local aristocracy.

At Newcastle digs have revealed postholes for timber structures as well as paving and a water supply. Some new purpose was evidently found for the site; the discovery of red deer antler suggests that there may have been an antler-carving workshop, often a feature of a high status site. The building was destroyed by fire; the excavation found signs that the posts were burnt while still upright.

At this time Benwell appears to have been the most important settlement in the area. The former fort at Newcastle may still have been an important residence or a focus for religious and political activity. The vast majority of forts abandoned by the Romans were completely forgotten. The presence of the river and its crossing point ensured the continued importance of Pons Aelius into the period that came to be known as the 'Dark Ages'. The memory of a fortification here survives in the 'chester' element of the later name for the settlement at Pons Aelius, Monkchester.

THE GHOST FORT

We can only make an educated guess concerning just what happened at the end of the Western Roman Empire but our excavations at the Castle Garth give concrete evidence for the way the fort decayed and how the buildings were dismantled, leaving only a few courses of stonework. Soil and building debris built up over the roads and pavements. Stone was taken from the walls and foundations as an easy source of building material for new structures. When stone is removed, 'robber trenches' are left behind and many have been found at the Newcastle fort.

Society of Antiquaries of Newcastle upon Tyne

This vertiginous photograph, taken from the top of the Keep, shows part of the central range of the Roman fort under excavation in 1979.

We can relate the wedge shape of the excavation to the plans on pages 43 and 53. A corner of the fort headquarters with strong room is central in the photograph. To its left is an alley, and then a wall of the commanding officer's house is visible. Later deposits and graves obscure the Roman remains.

RE-FOUNDED BY THE DEAD

During the construction of the railway across the Castle Garth in 1847, large quantities of human bone were uncovered. Local antiquarians assumed that it was a burial ground for the victims of the plague of 1638. Excavators looking for Roman remains in the 1920s uncovered more burials, but once it was established that they were not of Roman date, they were discarded as being too recent for serious study. It was not until the Castle Garth dig of the 1970s that the true significance of the cemetery was recognised, and the burials scientifically excavated.

The general date of the burial ground was soon apparent – the graves cut the Roman walls and were cut through by the Norman defences. Detailed examination of the skeletons has revealed a remarkable amount of information about life and death during this period – between AD 700 and 1100. 679 individuals were found during the excavations. This number reflects only a small proportion of the total cemetery population, as we have reason to believe the cemetery was originally bigger. In digging the foundations for the Norman castle, many graves were destroyed, and many more when the Victorian railway arches were built, but despite the losses, the Castle Garth has still produced the largest collection of pre-Norman burials in the North East.

In 1990 further excavations of the Saxon graves at Castle Garth were carried out by archaeologists.

The main difference we see is that earlier burial traditions, which left no trace of most of the population, have been replaced by burial in communal cemeteries in sacred places. The choice of this site is very significant – the ruins of the abandoned fort were still visible as the first graves were dug in the early 8th century. A reverence for the Roman Imperial past is seen in the fact that many former forts are chosen as locations for churches. The fact that this site overlooks the river, with its far earlier religious significance, may also show how the beliefs and lifestyles of the new society were meshed from a web of much older strands.

LAST RITES

The details of the skeletons and the way they were buried were carefully recorded in order to reveal as much as possible about the people interred here. All the bodies were buried in the Christian style, with the head of the body at the western end of the grave and feet to the east. The reason for this is that early Christians believed that on the Day of Judgement, the dead would rise up out of their graves facing towards the Holy City of Jerusalem.

Most were laid out straight and on their backs, some lay on their sides, others on their stomachs and a few were curled up. Grave goods were absent, unlike in earlier, pagan burials, as Christians did not believe that such goods were taken on to the afterlife.

The position of the bodies may reveal whether the corpse was enclosed in a coffin, wrapped in a shroud, or laid without covering. A cramped position for the arms and legs showed that the body was tightly bound in a shroud. A small number, less than ten, had pins that were holding the shroud in place. Twelve per cent of those excavated were buried in timber coffins. These were detected by the imprints of planks within the graves, or occasional fragments of wood that survived rusted to nails or other iron objects in the soil.

Shroud pins.

The graves themselves were shallow by modern standards, only 25cm to 60cm deep, and usually in straight lines or rows. Graves had been dug to avoid disturbing recent burials but the fact that so many graves cut into earlier burials suggests that there were few surface grave markers, to show where older burials lay. Two charnel pits, into which the disturbed bones were placed, were found in the cemetery. It was thought to be important to preserve as much as possible of the earthly remains of the person, otherwise the body could not be resurrected on Judgement Day and the soul would be lost.

MEDICAL MYSTERIES

Osteology is the study of bones. Through the condition of the bones, it is possible to learn about the make-up of the population and their lifestyle. The most basic data about a skeleton is its age and gender, but even these can be surprisingly problematic to establish. The rate of development of bones and the signs of a skeleton's gender, such as the width of the hipbone and the shape of the skull, vary greatly between individuals. It is almost impossible to assign a gender to

The larger skeleton here suffered from scoliosis, which causes a curvature of the spine and, in advanced cases like this, paralysis of the lower body. The skulls of these skeletons were removed by the digging of a later grave.

children as skeletal gender differences do not develop until adolescence, while pinpointing the age of an adult is very difficult as it must be based on the wear on the bones, rather than the obvious developmental stages that make children much easier to age accurately.

It is often assumed that people in the past were shorter than people today. From measurements of the skeletons, heights appear to range between 5ft 2ins-6ft for men and 4ft 7ins-5ft 7ins for women. Although they cannot match the tallest of modern people, the majority of early Christians would not stand out on a modern street just because of their height.

Joint diseases, osteoarthritis and osteoporosis were found to be common among the inhabitants of 8th and 9th century Newcastle. Some showed signs of dental abscesses, poor childhood nutrition (which leaves marks on the bones) and fractures. They are all common defects in skeletons from past ages – these problems seem to have plagued people for many centuries.

Along with the usual signs of disease, two very odd problems were found among the contemporary people of the area. Over twelve per cent of the bodies recovered in 1990-1992 had Spina Bifida, a birth defect that affects the nerves of the spine, and cause a variety of problems including partial paralysis. It is thought to be caused by some combinations of hereditary and environmental factors, but why this population had such a high number of cases is currently unexplained.

The second odd finding has the potential to overturn long-held ideas about the origins of a major disease. Three of the children displayed symptoms of congenital syphilis, namely 'mulberry molars', a condition where the surface of the molars is made of small lumps and resembles a mulberry. The disease is passed from an infected mother to her child while it is still in the womb and can often kill newborns. It can also strike much later and cause deformities, as was probably the case with these children. Their presence means there was at least one woman in the community (assuming they were siblings, more if they were not) who had contracted syphilis. This is remarkable because the disease is commonly thought to have been brought back from the Americas by the crews of Columbus' ships in 1492-3. These unlucky children are among the few, heavily disputed, examples of syphilis which pre-date this. If this discovery can be confirmed, it would mean the disease was present in Europe at least 500 years earlier than previously thought and raise questions about its origin in Europe.

EQUAL BEFORE GOD?

A few people had more elaborate graves. In some cases stones were placed on either side of the skull, possibly to prevent the head rolling sideways. Others had another stone added along the top of the head, then a final stone balanced across these three stones to create a box around the skull, to prevent it from being crushed. Five graves were lined with rubble, often from the surrounding fort and may have had a wooden lid placed across them, to make a simple tomb. Fifteen people were surrounded by stone slabs, creating cists.

Skeleton 605's skull was protected by a stone cover while 509 had a complete stone coffin.

Many of these different practices are probably the result of changing fashions rather than an indication of wealth or status. There are some clues to higher status burials in the grave yard, such as stone markers on the surface. These were all found to the south of the cemetery's church. This area was probably used only by the most important individuals in the local community. Occasionally, the remains of iron straps of the sort used to hold together household chests were found. It is known from other sites of this date that such chests were re-used as coffins, often for wealthy individuals.

One skeleton was found lying face down with its hands tied behind its back. This is often an indicator of execution or murder as it suggests the victim was bound before being killed, then tossed carelessly into their grave. Evidence of at least one violent death is provided by three sword cuts on the skull of a middle-aged man. The absence of healing shows that the individual died either from the blows or very soon after.

An artist's impression of a chest burial at the cemetery in around AD 900.

Some examples of the range of different grave markers used at the cemetery between AD 800 and 1100.

FROM GRAVEYARD TO CHURCHYARD

Along with the bodies, the remains of buildings were found within the bounds of the cemetery. The excavators worked out that these were almost certainly a pair of churches, designed to serve the cemetery. The earlier chapel was a simple rectangular stone building, similar to many 10th century churches consisting of only a single open room. Many new churches were built during the 10th century; in this case, it appears the local population felt it right to add a church to their well-established burial ground, perhaps to better

A millstone, possibly of Roman date, that has been re-used as a grave-cover and simply decorated with a Christian cross.

perform their funerary rites. A second building with a western tower replaced it. Measuring 22m by 4.5m, it is possible that this was in fact two churches sitting end to end, an arrangement found at other early ecclesiastical sites such as Jarrow and Whithorn. As is too often the case, the building remains were so disturbed that it is difficult be certain what the churches looked like.

Many burials of newborn and young children were clustered near the southern wall of the church. It was traditional to bury infants who died before baptism under the eaves of the church, where rain running off the holy building would drip upon them and perhaps baptise them after death, releasing their souls to heaven.

NORMAN TYNESIDE

A NEW AND BRUTAL REGIME

On 14th May, 1080, the most hated man in the North, William Walcher, the Norman bishop of Durham and Earl of Northumbria, came to Gateshead hoping to resolve a blood feud. The kinsmen of a Northumbrian nobleman murdered by one of Walcher's Norman knights were assembled to be addressed by Walcher. Inflamed by the presence of the murderer in Walcher's party and resentful after a decade of Norman oppression, the Northumbrians refused to be

St Mary's church, Gateshead, scene of the murder of Bishop Walcher.

placated by the saintly bishop. The mood turned murderous and the bishop's party had to seek refuge in the church of Saint Mary, which was then set alight, forcing the Normans out of hiding and to their deaths at the hands of the mob. Outside the doors of the church, and possibly within the encircling bank of the prehistoric enclosure, the bishop and all of his henchmen were slain. A brutal retaliation devastated the rebellious region and to maintain order and deter Scottish aggression King William's son, Robert Curthose, built a 'New Castle' commanding the river crossing and overlooking the scene of the murder.

The stone castle we see today is newer than the original New Castle, which would have been made of timber and earth. Early in the long excavation of the Castle Garth, the archaeologists hoped they would uncover some trace of the first castle before they dug down into the Roman fort beneath it. In 1973 they uncovered a small area of clay bank that seemed promising. Over the next three years, they were proved right as much more of the early castle's earthworks were revealed.

Judith Dobie

An artistic reconstruction of the wooden castle under construction in around 1080.

A small settlement has sprung up between the western and northern gates and the first riverside warehouses and workshops are appearing. Within the Castle Garth or yard the small church and its graveyard are still in use on ground where the stone Keep would come to be built.

THE OLD NEW CASTLE

This first castle (see the illustration opposite), like all early Norman castles, would have consisted of a wooden fence surrounding a stout wooden tower. Timber defences were more vulnerable to fire and blade than stone walls, but were quickly thrown up from materials readily to hand. The earthworks supplemented the already defensible nature of the site, with steep slopes to the east and south. What survived to be recorded by the excavators was a ditch, about 2m wide at the bottom, around a clay bank which would have supported a defensive wall made of close-set timbers with sharpened ends. The surviving inner bank was about 7m higher than the base of the ditch, a formidable distance for a besieging force to scale while under heavy fire.

To date, nothing more than the bank and ditch of the castle have been uncovered, and so our reconstruction is based on other examples of this type of Norman castle. Within the ring work, the cemetery church remains in use and outside the main entrance, before the Black Gate was built, the small houses of the first townsfolk are beginning to spring up.

The second most important building, after the timber keep, was the great hall, which was where the Vermont Hotel now stands. The great hall would have been the real heart of the castle as the lord's day-to-day home, rather than the cramped Keep. In a time when the whole population was devoutly Christian, the castle church provided the necessary services to the people living there. The other buildings are kitchens, bakeries, breweries, workshops, stables and stores, all vital for feeding and supporting the castle.

The excavation has found that the presence of the graves in the cemetery didn't stop the building of the castle on the promontory. From both structural evidence and radio-carbon dating, we know that the section of the cemetery around the church was still in use when the Normans decided to build a castle on top of it. Indeed, burial continued after construction began. The workers who put in the massive foundations for the Keep must have been constantly digging through human skeletons, but this did not seem to deter the Norman

Excavating the castle ditch at the Black Gate in the 1970s.

engineers. There is no record of how the local people felt about their burial ground being violated to provide a castle for a foreign prince. All we know is that burials in Castle Garth ceased as the castle became established, probably when replacement churches were available in the new town. Both St Andrew's Church on Newgate Street and St Nicholas Cathedral have masonry dating to this early period in the history of the town.

AT THE BOTTOM OF THE MOAT

Though the ditch was intended as a defence, it inevitably attracted a certain amount of rubbish dumping. In the towns of the Middle Ages, rubbish was often thrown onto gardens or just into the street, which resulted, over the centuries, in the ground level rising by as much as ten or twelve feet in places like York and London. Although this added to the stench and disease of medieval towns, archaeologists have benefitted from being able to study large quantities of finds relating to the everyday life of the townspeople. In Newcastle however, we don't see this large build-up of waste material across the town centre, and it seems that the inhabitants of both town and castle were encouraged, or compelled, to dump their rubbish at specific locations, known as middens. Households near the river may have tipped directly onto the foreshore, or directly into the river, as part of a deliberate programme to reclaim land from the water in order to construct shipping quays.

'Quarrels', iron cross-bow bolt tips, from the castle ditch.

It took a long while for the dumping of rubbish to start at the castle ditch. While the wooden castle had been built at the end of the 11th century, the first layers of rubbish dated to the 13th century. In order to keep the ditch in defensive use, it was either kept clean of rubbish, or cleaned out regularly. As a result, there are few Norman finds from the excavations. Among the most interesting discoveries are a group of iron cross-bow bolt tips – known as 'quarrels'. When

The sole of a Norman shoe from the castle ditch.

64

found, it was assumed they dated to the later years of the castle, but the careful excavations here have shown that they represent a very early use of the most up-to-date weapons – cross-bows – by the King's garrison at the New Castle.

Many more mundane objects reveal the life of the soldiers and their families. The sole of a Norman shoe was retrieved from the bottom of the ditch. There was enough left to identify it as the sole of a right foot turnshoe. Turnshoes were a common style throughout the Middle Ages and were so-called because they were inside out when they were stitched together, then turned the right way out when they were finished.

Digging in the moat. The Norman curtain wall of the castle is top left. The archaeologist at the back of the dig is measuring and drawing the layers the cut has revealed. In the foreground the archaeologists are trowelling through deposits. A modern drainage pipe has cut right through the Norman wall. This would not be allowed to happen now as the castle is a scheduled ancient monument.

MAKING A MARK

The next defining event in the life of the castle was its rebuilding in stone at the command of Henry II, beginning in 1167 and taking over ten years. The result was the Keep which still stands today. The expense was great as each stone was hand cut by skilled masons. Masons' pay was based on how much stone they cut. To prove to their supervisors how much work was theirs, each mason would incise his own distinctive symbol onto his stones. These masons' marks can still be seen in the castle and in many other medieval stone buildings. We know that the supervising mason was called Maurice – his family settled in the town and became wealthy enough to own property and take part in town affairs. He later went on to design Dover Castle, in a similar style to the Keep at Newcastle, but

A mason's mark from the Chapel.

on a slightly larger scale. It was part of the seven great castle-building projects of Henry II, which produced, for example, the castles at Windsor, Scarborough and Nottingham.

There would have been a great deal more to the stone castle than we see today. Our reconstruction is based on a combination of documentary records and archaeological evidence. An excavation in 1961 next to the Bridge Hotel found a section of the southern curtain wall partly covered over by later layers. Above the ground, the South Gate, overlooking the river, and, most importantly, the Keep itself, have survived from this early period.

To King Henry, the New Castle was a key part of the defence of his kingdom, a formidable fortress to protect the river crossing and to bar the road to the south to the king's enemies. It was also the place where he would meet with the envoys of the Scottish crown and receive submission from the often independently minded Northern nobles.

His architect, Maurice the Engineer, took great care to plan the building to fulfil these roles. The only access to the Keep was by the main staircase (at the foremost corner) which was approached through a gatehouse tower, now gone, but shown on 19th century views. The stairs were steep, long and narrow and designed to over awe and intimidate visitors

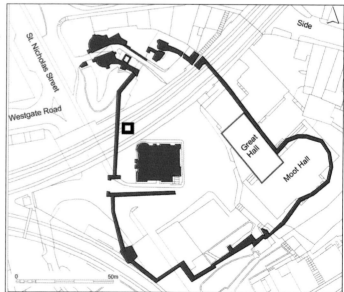

A plan of the early Keep and its wall in the mid-13th century.

In this cutaway we can see how thick the walls of the Keep needed to be to contain the passages and stairways required for soldiers to move around the building. The original roof was of wooden rafters. The present day stone vault of the Keep, and the corner turrets and flag tower were added when the building was restored in 1811.

with the power of the monarch. They led, through an ornate doorway with two massive timber and iron doors, directly into the Great Hall. This space was open from floor to timber roof – the round arched ceiling that we see now is a Victorian alteration. Attached to the hall was the 'King's Chamber', (seen on page 67 in cross-section, in the near left-hand wall) the castle's principal apartment, with its own fireplace and toilet. The large opening visible in the rear wall of the hall led to a small chamber thought to be the castle prison. On the floor below is a smaller hall, which would have provided accommodation to the more lowly residents of the castle. The 'Queen's Chamber' is another private chamber, in the rear wall beneath the prison. Beneath this was another floor at the bottom of the spiral staircase, made up of the Keep's chapel and a large storeroom. Although it cannot be seen here, the Keep also has its own well, a convenient water source for daily life and an absolute necessity if the Keep were besieged.

The chapel before its 19th century restoration.

Some everyday objects found in the Castle Garth, and now on display in the Keep.

A jet spindle.

Part of a belt buckle.

Dice, made by simply punching the pips into cubes of bone.

In addition to the grand chambers of the stone Keep, the separate great hall still stood within the outer bailey, built against the curtain wall. Medieval kings constantly travelled about their country. They would move between their castles or stay with local lords or monks, dragging their entire court along with them. The king would deal with the local business and enjoy the local hospitality before moving on. And the local business at Newcastle was particularly important – it was where the English and Scottish kings would meet. Henry III and Alexander II negotiated there in 1236, while in 1292 Edward I, 'The Hammer of the Scots', received an oath of loyalty from John Baliol. The castle was a fit meeting ground for two European heads of state.

Society of Antiquaries of Newcastle upon Tyne

The Keep in the early 13th century.

THE MEDIEVAL TOWN OF NEWCASTLE

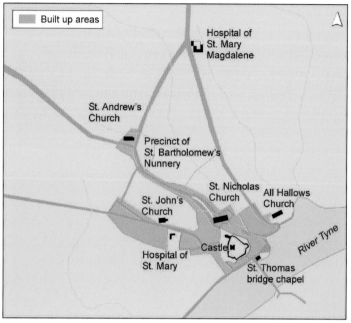

Above, the early medieval town.

In much the same way as the vicus grew up around the Roman fort, a town quickly began to spring up around the castle. Within a hundred years a large urban centre had become established, including four parish churches, numerous markets, and a new bridge, built on the same site as the modern Swing Bridge. The waterfront and the town's dramatic street pattern, imposed on the inhabitants by the steep slopes and ravines of the cliff side, would have been the defining features of the urban landscape and have been explored through excavations at Stockbridge, Newcastle, and Bottle Bank, Gateshead.

Right, an excavation at Tuthill Stairs on the Close.
The excavators are in the process of undercovering a medieval building constructed on reclaimed land. Beneath the houses, a wooden waterfront was discovered showing the position of the original riverbank.

BANKS OF BALLAST

The waterfront has been the subject of many excavations over the past fifty years. The site of the ancient waterfront is now well inland, because most of what is now the East Quayside and all of the Close has been reclaimed from the river. In about a quarter of all archaeological trenches in Newcastle, nearly forty in all, the riverbed is found at the bottom of the trench. From these we know that the earliest land reclamation was in the 12th century and this activity peaked between the 13th and 15th centuries. The demand for more quays and better facilities steadily transformed the riverside from its natural shape into its modern form.

The 13th century river wall at Stockbridge. The timber riverfront was replaced by hardier stone walls to create a more solid bank. The stone steps provided access to the river itself. The number on the board is the riverfront's 'context number' – everything found on an excavation is numbered to help in recording the site.

Reclamation was carried out by building a wall in the river and dumping landfill or ballast behind it to the desired level. Ballast is the term for any heavy material placed in the hold of a ship when it lacks cargo, as the weight is required for the ship to sit properly in the water – a very light ship would be at risk of capsizing. The ballast would then be dumped when the ship reached its destination and was filled up with cargo.

The later medieval town, with the outline of the town walls.

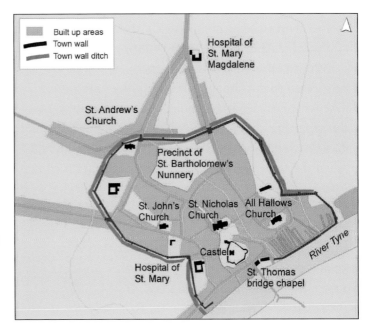

Here this otherwise worthless material was put to use. Examining the geology in the gravel has revealed some of it came from the Thames estuary. Rubbish and building debris from the town was also used to build up the ground surface, exactly like modern land reclamations using landfill.

The conditions created by dumping rubbish in the river are very useful to archaeologists. Under most conditions leather rots, leaving nothing for archaeological recovery. However, in extremely wet conditions, there is not enough oxygen to support the bacteria that would break down the leather.

A 13th century timber drain from Stockbridge. The woodwork provides evidence of contemporary methods of carpentry. The planks are held together by wooden dowel pegs.

Without these bacteria, the leather can survive for centuries. Such conditions were found in waterfront excavations at Queen Street. Here, pieces of belt, a knife sheath, scraps, offcuts and several complete shoes were found. Most were ankle boots, fastened with either a metal buckle and strap or with laces along the sides. Two had woven straw matting inside the soles, for warmth or comfort. So much leather was found at this site that it is suspected that a shoemaker or cobbler had a workshop here. These were two separate trades: shoemakers were forbidden from repairing shoes, while cobblers were not allowed to make shoes. As well as hosting the shoe trade, the reclaimed land pushed the waterfront forward into deeper areas of the river,

Seeds and plant remains from a waterlogged site.

allowing larger ships to dock there. At Stockbridge, waterlogged deposits preserved several wooden drains which contained organic rubbish used by inhabitants as well as seeds and plant remains from the surrounding environment.

Again it is the importance of the river that drives the development of the town – now as the port for a growing merchant community. In another hundred years, Newcastle would be the most important port on the British side of the North Sea, after London.

DIGGING UP STOCKBRIDGE

In 1995, Newcastle's largest waterfront excavation was carried out along Blyth Nook, behind the Crown Courts. In medieval times, this was the site of the Stock Bridge. The name comes from a bridge that crossed Pandon Dene and hosted a stockfish market.

Beneath the foundations of 19th and 20th century, the first significant remains were stone buildings from the 15th and 16th centuries. These were the most recent in a sequence of medieval buildings stretching back to the 13th century. All these buildings appear to have been used as smithies, judging by their well-used hearths, the large quantities of ash and metal-working

Above, a general view of the excavations at Stockbridge. The dig revealed both the Pandon Burn, which has been hidden under the industrial buildings since the 18th century, and the medieval road across the burn. Right, a close up of the medieval road at Blyth Nook.

waste. As far as we can tell, the living quarters were on the first floor, to allow as much space as possible at ground level for industrial and commercial activity. The persistence of the iron-working industry on this site shows how important an industrial distinct Pandon had become. The shallow banks of the stream were the site of the earliest ship-building yards in the town   in 1294 King Edward I commissioned a galley to be built there, in preparation for war with Scotland. The ship became known as the Pandon Galley and its records mention iron being brought from as far as Spain for the project, as demand exceeded local supply. The riverside industries boomed during the Scottish Wars.

The earliest stone waterfront was found at Stockbridge, complete with a flight of stairs down to the river. The very first sign of human occupation was the creation of the land itself, in the late 12th or early 13th century. A fence of wattle (woven sticks) formed the new

Keys found at Stockbridge.

riverbank, with rubbish, stones and soil dumped behind it. The waterlogged soil had preserved the wood, as well as pieces of leather and cloth. In the first couple of centuries of its existence, wool was the port's main export – low quality fleece from the Pennine and Cheviot hill sheep – and it was only later, in the 14th century, that the town's defining product, black, shiny coal, was an important commodity.

At the very bottom of the sequence of layers was the original bank of Pandon Burn, a broad, shallow stream that once fed into the Tyne.

Some of the Stockbridge finds uncover a lighter, more musical side to life in medieval Pandon. A set of bone tuning pegs for a zither (a relative of the guitar) was found, stained green by the copper wire of the strings once wrapped around them. Two bone whistles and a mouthpiece of a woodwind instrument were also recovered. Musicians commonly worked around dockside inns and bathhouses during the medieval period, as they were busy spots filled with sailors in search of entertainment in their brief time ashore. Brothels too were common by the waterfront, again to meet the demands of the sailors and

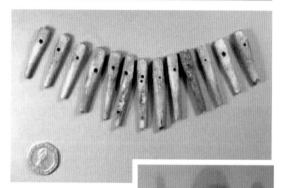

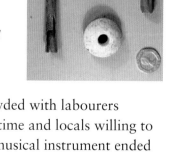

Top, excavating a hearth at Stockbridge. Above, bone tuning pegs for a zither. Right, two bone whistles and two spindle whorls.

visiting tradesmen. The narrow streets of the waterfront would have been crowded with labourers moving cargo to the markets, bickering merchants, sailors in search of a good time and locals willing to give it to them for a price. We will never know quite how several shoes and a musical instrument ended up abandoned in the reclamation tips, but it does sound like it was an amazing night out on the Quayside.

THE BISHOP'S MANOR

Life in Gateshead was a little quieter, and it is during this period that disputes between the merchants of Newcastle and Gateshead become a common occurrence. The presence of the Royal Castle on the Newcastle side, which the king needed to keep strong as a buttress against the Scots, meant the monarch always sided with Newcastle.

Most of the land on the south side of the river was granted to the Bishops of Durham. Their manor stretched over almost all of eastern Gateshead and contained a valuable forest, with a manor house on the site of Park House and a bishop's residence at the southern end of Oakwellgate. A fast-growing town developed along the approach to the bridge. St Mary's church in its present form was built in around 1200, upon the site of the earlier church that was either destroyed or badly damaged when Bishop Walcher met his death. The streets have a regular grid pattern during the 12th century, which suggests that the Bishop or the burgesses might have attempted to control the growth of the town by laying out a regular pattern of building plots for the inhabitants to construct their houses and workshops.

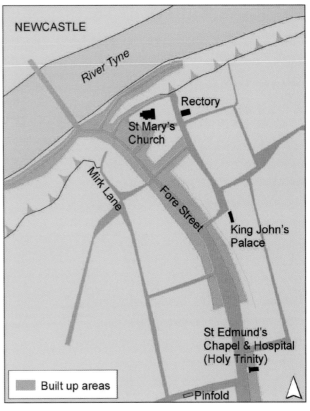

Gateshead in the 12th century.

Excavations within the graveyard at St Mary's church, Gateshead.

MEDIEVAL BOTTLE BANK

Like most medieval towns, Newcastle and Gateshead were a patchwork of narrow building plots known as 'burgage' plots – owned or rented by a 'burgher' or property-holder in the town. They were long strips of land with a house or shop facing onto the street, and a back yard and garden beyond. The boundaries of burgage plots are often preserved to the present day, because generations of owners have rebuilt on the same area. This was the case at Bottle Bank, Gateshead, excavated in 2000. Here the streets and yards had the same layout as the medieval plots first divided up in the 12th or 13th century.

The owners of the plots had found numerous ways of marking out their property. Stake holes indicated early wattle fences, which were replaced with stone walls in the 14th century. The houses on the street front were destroyed by later rebuilding, but the remains of the foundations of buildings were found in the yards and gardens, usually they were utility buildings such as brewhouses and workshops. At the rear of the tenement, pits were dug as the most convenient means of disposing of unpleasant waste. They were more often placed near the boundaries of the plots, leaving the centre clear for other

Right, this 13th century cess pit at Bottle Bank was lined with woven sticks known as wattle which have survived remarkably well. It had been used for many years to dispose of human waste.

Below, a 13th century well which has been sectioned mechanically.

uses – horticulture, workshops, pens for animals etc. As pits filled up, they would be covered over with soil and a new pit dug elsewhere on the property. The most common pits found at Bottle Bank were cesspits, a necessity prior to sewer systems. Others contained domestic and kitchen waste such as ashes and large quantities of bone. Fortunately for archaeologists, broken pottery would also be dumped in these pits, allowing the period of usage to be dated through pottery styles. Other remnants of everyday life turned up too, such as knives, keys, scraps of children's shoes and three wooden bowling balls, used in games resembling skittles or bowls.

IN THE STREETS: GALLOWGATE

A substantial excavation of medieval Newcastle took place in 2003 on a site beneath Gallowgate bus station. This part of Gallowgate had been cleared of buildings when the town walls were built in the early 1280s, to leave a 'bow-shot length' between the nearest buildings and the walls and turrets of the town's new protective barrier.

Simple medieval houses and shops were laid out in burgage plots, which had yards and gardens behind the houses. From the remains in one of the rubbish pits, it seems that one of the shops was a cobbler's.

By AD 1200, Newcastle was expanding along the reclaimed riverside, with its new harbour,

The medieval street, Gallowgate (named because the town gibbet, where bodies of executed prisoners were displayed, lay further along the road on a hill overlooking the town) lies to the top of this photograph.

and along major routes north, east and west to the towns of Morpeth, North Shields and Carlisle. Excavations in the town centre have produced pottery, animal remains and industrial debris.

Pottery was manufactured on the East Quayside where Blue Anchor Yard now stands and in the 12th century the town was a major centre for pottery and iron goods.

The town also began to see the establishment of religious houses. The Dominican monastery of Blackfriars, established in 1239, was investigated in the 1970s and again during building work for the Gate cinema and entertainment complex development on Low Friar Street. An almost complete medieval pot was recovered from the excavation.

A closer view of medieval houses on Gallowgate. On the left we can see the foundations of the houses, and the paved back yards are to the right.

Left, an 18th century view of the buildings of Blackfriars monastery and right, an almost complete pot that was excavated from the site.

THE EMERGENCE OF A REGIONAL CAPITAL

By the start of the 12th century we can see Newcastle as a town bursting with life and opportunity, with all the basic features that will allow it to grow into a major urban centre. It is on its way to self-governance and has four churches, clear street layouts that are home to an ever growing population and a busy port on the river Tyne. In contrast to Newcastle's wealth Gateshead is just beginning as an urban settlement. It had plans to rebuild its church and has early signs of a street plan. At this time Gateshead's biggest asset was the bridge over the river, linking it to the world beyond.

From Newcastle and Gateshead's earliest origins it was the junction of river and road that provided the focus for all later activity. As we come to the end of the early history, the town of Newcastle is at the point of transformation that took it from being just another port on the eastern seaboard, to the pre-eminent centre in the north, the King's regional capital. After a long period of relative peace and prosperity through the 12th and well into the 13th century, storm clouds gathered on the northern horizon, and the next hundred years were marked by war, plague and border strife. The town braced itself for hard times and wrapped its streets and churches in stone walls with high towers. When conditions settled again, it was the river that carried the town into a new realm of international commerce and coal-based industrial expansion and a new identity as the North Sea Capital.

An imaginary view of Newcastle in the 16th century by artist Byron Dawson.

THE STORY GOES ON ...

The First Natives of this Island.

THe Britains were *Antochthenes*, Natives of this Island, for more Ancient Inhabitants we finde none. The People of this Nation is thought to have been descended from the Neighbouring *Gaules*, in regard of the same Religion, Language, and Manners. Their Originall from the Trojans by *Brute* is altogether fabulous; there being no Greek or Latine Authors, or any Monument in this Island which makes mention hereof. Their Descent from the *Gaules* is more probable, being the next parts of the Continent unto Britaine, or their way from *Asia* or the East, from whence all Countries was first Peopled.

From 'Chorographia', William Grey's Survey of Newcastle upon Tyne, 1649.

THE FUTURE OF OUR PAST

When the first History of Newcastle was written by William Grey in 1649, nothing was known about the earliest times, what we call 'prehistory', but he did understand that the river was the life-blood of Newcastle and Gateshead, and he also knew that the past was all-important in shaping the character of the present. Almost all of Grey's information came from documents and, while they are important sources of information, we are increasingly reliant on excavation and finds research to illuminate the darker recesses of history. It is probably true to say that we have learned more in the last 40 years than in the three centuries between Grey's time and the first excavations of the modern period. The pace has quickened over the past ten years, and, as the process of redevelopment continues, excavation in advance of re-building will continue to throw-up new discoveries.

Every year there are several sites in Newcastle and Gateshead that require excavation before redevelopment. It is pure chance whether or not ancient remains survive. A dig on the former Parcels Office in 2010 was in a key location at the bottom of Westgate Road, between the Vicus and Hadrian's Wall. It is an intriguing location. Did the civilian settlement run right up to the Wall – was there a

Courtesy North Pennines Archaeology

Courtesy Ian Farmers Associates (1998) Ltd

Left, the dig at the former Parcels Office, Westgate Road, 2010. Right, and below, locating the Roman Wall (including an interesting carved symbol) under a back garden in Benwell.

market place between, or was it another area, like Clavering Place, given over to burying the dead? Unfortunately, Victorian cellars on the site have destroyed all traces of earlier remains, and so nothing new was learned.

By contrast, at Benwell, in the back garden of a 1930s house built on top of the Roman fort (Condercum), stone buildings were discovered immediately below the surface of the lawn. The wall was part of one of the military buildings, possibly a granary, including a carving on one of the blocks which may be a phallic fertility or good-luck symbol.

Courtesy Ian Farmers Associates (1998) Ltd

Archaeology is a hit and miss affair, but we must be constantly vigilant to preserve important sites and excavate areas which do not merit preservation but which can tell us about the past lives of the people of Tyneside.

Less than one per cent of Newcastle and Gateshead has been archaeologically excavated and many of our most important digs were done without the benefit of modern scientific techniques. Sites in the 1970s and 1980s were investigated before the advent of palaeo-environmental sampling. Dating methods improve year by year, and the use of digital recording of sites and buildings is revolutionising archaeological techniques. For example, it is now possible to record the outside of a historic building in more detail in an hour with a laser scanner that could be done in a week of measuring and drawing. A recent example is the north side of the Black Gate, where it is proposed to build a new lift, as part of a wider programme to transform the visitor facilities at the Castle and Cathedral.

And equally important is the need to promote and publicise the history of the area. This book makes a small contribution to that end, complementing the work of Tyne and Wear Archives and Museums, the Heritage and Library Services of the two councils and the work of local societies.

*From 'Chorographia', William Grey's History
of Newcastle, 1649.*

The archaeologist above is using a traditional technique called 'flotation'. Soil is put into a net in a container of water. The heavy soil will sink leaving lighter fragments floating on the surface.

The latest technology – a laser scan of the Black Gate.

Index of places mentioned